FEAR OF
COMPUTERS

FEAR OF COMPUTERS

Written and Illustrated by

Michael Cohn

Northwest Publishing Inc.
Salt Lake City, Utah

Fear of Computers

A small portion of this book is based on articles
by the author and originally published in Computerworld
(copyright 1987 by CW Publishing, Inc., 375 Cochituate Rd.,
Framingham, MA 01701; reprinted from Computerworld).

PRINTING HISTORY
First Printing 1994

ISBN: 1-56901-230-X

NPI books are published by Northwest Publishing, Incorporated,
5949 South 350 West, Salt Lake City, Utah 84107.
The name "NPI" and the "NPI" logo are trademarks belonging to
Northwest Publishing, Incorporated.

PRINTED IN THE UNITED STATES OF AMERICA.
10 9 8 7 6 5 4 3 2 1

With heartfelt thanks to Terri.

Table of Contents

Foreword

I first encountered Michael Cohn five years ago when he was a successful computer salesman struggling to make it as a humor writer. I don't know what it was about Mike—his razor wit, his deep insight, his technological savvy—but somehow, just somehow I knew that Mike had the one thing it took to make it in publishing: he would work for less than $500.

Now, despite the fact that he has been frequently published in *Computerworld,* Mike has landed a book contract. And I'm proud to think that *Computerworld* played some small part in launching the career of the man who is certainly the greatest humorist in the computer industry. In fact, he is the *only* humorist in the computer industry.

You need to understand that computer people are not known for having a great sense of humor. A typical joke among computer people would be something like:

"Knock knock."

"Who's there?"

"Redirector."

"Redirector who?"

"Redirect'er over to me. I have a remote procedure call in my pocket."

(Peals of uncontrolled laughter)

Certainly there is a yawning void for Mike Cohn to fill. And fill it he does with an engaging and sympathetic style that recognizes that deep down, people really have love-hate affairs with their computers. The best thing about Cohn is that he doesn't just laugh at technology itself, but at the strange things that technology makes people do. Cohn recognizes that in these primordial days of computing we call the '90s, humans are basically struggling to get machines that can't think to act like people should act. The fact that those machines continually confound us in that pursuit by doing exactly what we tell them to do, instead of what we want them to do, is an endless source of amusement to him. Cohn excels at his craft because he knows just enough about computer technology to understand how limited it is and he's been around people long enough to know just how silly their reactions to those limits can be.

Take a cruise through Cohn's world and see if you don't agree. For a shade less than $500, he comes cheap. For what you just paid, he's a steal.

Paul Gillin, Editor
Computerworld

ONE

You Are Not Alone

There's something going on here. Something terrible. Something frightening. There are menaces all around us, and every day it's getting worse.

They're at your office. They're in your house. I'm sure you've seen them. They're square. They beep. They're computers, and they inflict unspeakable pain. Yet no one's in much of a hurry to do anything about them...no one has tried to stop the spread of data processing.

Computers are scary. They're confusing. They cost a lot.

Even worse, they're all over the place...still we keep making more. And strangely enough, this bothers only a handful of us, those of us who have a fear of computers.

If you fear computers, you are not alone. Lots of folks hate them. Plenty of people won't even go near them. But each day this gets harder and harder, as high-tech infects every corner of the globe.

Within ten years, scientists predict there will be more computers in this country than people. We're being outnumbered; even surrounded! The prospect is frightening. What if all these computers get a little fussy? Or angry? Or want the right to vote?

The notion has kept me awake more nights than I care to remember. Even more worrisome is the fact that most computers tend to attract computer-people, and computer-people are *really* scary.

They used to be easy to spot, with their thick glasses and white socks. Now they're disguised. They look like the rest of us. Business people use computers. Housewives use computers. Wake up, because even children are using computers! We keep kids away from beer, drugs, and cigarettes, but they're running around the schools of this nation with diskettes and keyboards and lord knows what else.

Computers will ruin your life if you let them. You can keep fighting, and try to live computer-free. But my guess is it's just too late. Computers have come too far. The plain truth is you're going to have to accept computers. You must either learn how to use them, or learn how to use the people who use them.

This book is a survival manual. I offer a simple method to transform yourself from a fearful, naive, happy computer illiterate to an experienced, miserable and financially-devastated computer user.

I am not an expert. I don't know all the facts, components, or capacities of computers. In fact, half the time I make them up. But I do know about the dangers of high-tech…about the harsh, complex inter-relationships between computers, computer users, and the people who sell them, especially if you're trying to return one without a receipt.

Somehow you've held out till now, struggling with your fear of computers. Let me help you. Let me carefully, gently take you across the high-tech threshold, into the world of computers. There may be some pain. There will be some expense. And perhaps some sweat, and tears, and long nights in front of the keyboard.

But in the end, you'll thank me. I've helped thousands of people shed their fear of computers. Well, maybe it only seems like thousands. Actually, I've only helped my boss, and some lady in Accounting, except she now works in the cafeteria serving side orders of vegetables…she says it's not *all* my fault.

So sit back, relax, and let me dispel your fear of computers.

You'll feel better about all this high-tech stuff in no time. Of course, before starting any computer program, please consult your physician.

Let's begin.

TWO

Where Did All These Darn Computers Come From?

Computers wouldn't seem all that scary if you knew how they got here in the first place. What you might need is a revealing, brief, and comparatively inaccurate history of computers, big and small, and the big and small fortunes made because of them.

The First Computer

Scientists, archeologists, and historians argue about what

actually constituted the first computer. Then again, scientists, archeologists, and historians probably argue about everything, including where to go for lunch.

There are many conflicting theories...was the human hand the first computer? Or what about toes? When the Chinese invented the first clock in 3000 BC, was that a computer? And how could they tell if it was a couple minutes fast?

There is evidence of computer-like figures in Egyptian hieroglyphics from 1500 BC. This might seem rather startling, except historians contend they're just VCR's. And centuries earlier, Oriental cave drawings depict interaction with computer-shaped objects...these probably were the folks making the VCR's.

However, the consensus among scientists today is that the abacus was the first computer. Partially because the abacus was the first true arithmetic device. Partially because the abacus was the first calculating tool with moving parts.

And partially because the first time somebody dropped one, those little beads probably shot in twenty different directions, and the abacus became the first computer to go down.

The Renaissance

During the Renaissance, there was a lot of very intellectual stuff going on, and people kind of figured the first real automated computer would be invented "any day now"...some even went out and bought little computer tables.

But, as it turned out, people were too busy painting and sculpting and writing music and waiting for someone to invent the radio. Alas, no computers. A couple of longhairs did come up with a primitive adding machine and a slide-rule or two, but without commercials on late night TV, they didn't even sell half a dozen.

The 1870s

Alexander Graham Bell gets a lot of press for inventing the telephone. But few people know that he actually invented the both the computer *and* the telephone. Tragically, history misquoted the greatest moment in communications; what Bell *really* said: "Mr. Watson, come here, I want you...the system's down again."

☺

The U.S. Census

America was growing like gangbusters at the turn of the century. There were people everywhere; crowding into cities, farming, moving West...and still it was impossible to find a fourth for Bridge.

In the meantime, the folks at the Census Bureau were doing everything by hand, and theirs were pretty full. They were supposed to count the population every ten years. But by the time they finished, it was time to start all over again...reminds me of my kid cleaning his room.

So this inventor named Herman Hollerith came up with a pretty good idea: first build a huge, complex, automated tabulating machine, then rent it to the Census Bureau, and finally, somehow figure out a way to get it downstairs from his third-story apartment.

The idea worked like a charm, the Bureau knew how many people were in America, and Hollerith was able to sock-away a large down payment on a new Ford roadster, in case someone were to invent one.

Unfortunately, Hollerith failed to become a household name, probably because folks were too fixated on all the other industrial revolution inventions of the time, like Pez. All right, maybe they didn't make Pez a hundred years ago...it only tastes like it.

The First Electronic Computers

Nothing speeds up the evolution of technology like a good war. In the 1940s, European engineers raced to build a computer that could unscramble messages and decipher enemy code. But only the Germans were sufficiently advanced to produce electronic computer printout. In 1945, a machine in Berlin spit out the first printed computer statement: "Get me out of here, I think we're losing."

The First American Computers

Soon after WWII, electronic computers became commercially viable in the U.S. Unfortunately, they were tremendously expensive, and as big as a basketball court. But American business needed computers to solve perplexing computer problems—like where to put the computer.

The Fifties

Computers got smarter. A computer was finally able to beat a human being in Chess. But ten minutes later, the computer proved no match for that same human being and a sledgehammer.

The Sixties

Computers got a little smaller, but the number of computer buyers got a lot bigger. Businesses clamored to gain advantage by installing computers before their competitors. By 1964, there were over 500 computers in the state of California.

Unfortunately, the only programmers around were three guys from a Junior College in Sacramento, who basically held the state's high-tech industry hostage, while spending all their earnings on cheap beer.

The Early Seventies

The first pocket calculator was invented. But the devices took a while to catch on, since everyone was losing theirs, or crushing it while doing "the Bump."

Few people also realize that in 1973, a sophomore at Iowa State invented the first commercially-viable PC on his kitchen counter, years ahead of anyone else. However, one fateful Friday night, one of his poker-buddies mistook the machine for a microwave oven, and doused both the device and the kid's future in eight ounces of Cheese Whiz.

The Eighties

The decade started with the industry in full stride. PC's were everywhere. High-tech salesmen raked-in a bundle. Computer programmers made more than lawyers. Silicon Valley realtors drove German sedans.

Computers became commonplace. There were ATM's. Grocery-store scanners. Phones were answered by computers. And kids preferred Nintendo to playing ball with Dad, 4-to-1.

But during the late eighties, bad things started happening to computer companies. Maybe the economy went bad. Maybe competition cut into profits. Maybe folks OD'ed on PacMan.

Whatever the case, high-tech took a nose-dive. Businesses downsized from mainframes to PC's. Programmers downsized to Toyota Tercels. Sure, people were still interested in computers, but computers just couldn't compete with the newer intellectual pastimes, like bungee jumping or watching professional wrestling.

Computers Today

Today, the computer industry is too small. The number of still-in-business computer companies is too small. The average computer programmer's raise is too small. And worst of all, computers are too small.

What used to fit on your desk now fits in your lap, or your palm, or your purse. Some of them don't even need keyboards... they're supposed to recognize my handwriting. That will be a feat, since most of the time *I* can't even recognize my handwriting.

Today's computers are just too tiny, just like those pesky pocket calculators. My guess is we'll start misplacing them again, or mistake them for the VCR remote. Which means that someday you'll lose thousands of dollars in computer equipment between the cushions of the family-room couch.

The Future

I'm reluctant to forecast what the future holds for the computer industry. But I'll give it a shot, since it can't be more off-base than the last three high-tech "predictions" I got sucked into by my stockbroker.

High-tech will be expected, abundant, and cheap. Devices will be the size of watches and fountain pens, and will all be activated by voice commands. This will make life tremendously convenient, except no one will know if the passenger in seat 24C is working on a computer spreadsheet, or just another weirdo.

But the future will belong to computers, and you'd better stop being scared, and start getting ready. Because the com-

puter-literate kids of today will become the automated genera-
tion of tomorrow...and if you want to compete with them,
you'd better know their terminology, understand their computers, and at least be able to free a Starship Princess from an
army of Inter-Galactic Ninja Dragon-beasts.

THREE

The Scary Things That Make Up Your Computer

When it comes to computers, there are hundreds of companies. There are thousands of models. There are millions of salesmen. It can get pretty intimidating, especially if you were just heading to Wal-Mart to see what you could get for twenty bucks.

But don't get scared. Don't be confused. Basically, there are only two types of computers:

1. the computers that are easy to use, and
2. the computers your boss wants you to use.

Of course, some folks like to get fairly technical and talk about chips, and MIPS, and megabytes, and memory…but 99% of these folks are either salesmen, or people who follow you around at parties.

So don't bother with all the technical stuff. In high-tech, there's really only one rule:

"The bigger the computer, the greater the odds you should have bought a smaller computer."

Keeping that in mind, you might want to have some idea what actually makes up a computer. You may want to buy one some day. Or you may need to know about them at work. Then again, maybe no one will ever say, "Hey Billy-bob, finish flipping them last four burgers, then get over there and re-boot that file server." But it's good to at least know *something* about computers…like not to drop one on your foot.

So, here's a little information about all the different parts that come with a computer, whether you know what to do with them or not:

The Screen

This one is pretty easy. With most computers, there's usually something that looks like a TV, except it probably doesn't have a coat hanger taped to the back to pick-up UHF.

This is the screen, which computer experts sometimes call

the "monitor," "Video Display Terminal (VDT)," or the "little box on top of the computer." What the screen is supposed to do is display the letters, numbers, and symbols you typed while using the keyboard. What the screen doesn't do is display the letters, numbers, and symbols you *tried* to type while using the keyboard.

The Keyboard

The keyboard closely resembles a typewriter, and is located somewhere below the screen. If you find something

about the size of a TV Dinner in front of your PC, it's safe to assume it's your keyboard... unless it's got separate little areas for peas and apple cobbler.

You may also spot some strange keys you'll never see on a typewriter, such as F4, NumLk, Alt, etc. Don't worry about these, you'll probably never hit them...unless you slam your forehead on the keyboard after trying for 35 minutes to get the screen to say anything besides "BAD COMMAND OR FILE NAME."

By the way, there's usually a little telephone cord running out of the keyboard, this is how most keyboards interface with the computer. And about the forehead banging…this is how most people interface with the computer.

The System Unit

Now if you're talking about PC's, you've probably got a system unit somewhere. This is generally the thing that isn't the screen and isn't the keyboard.

The system unit is the most expensive part of the computer, that's because it's where computers do all their thinking. I don't know why they can't do it in the shower, like everyone else.

Anyway, the system unit is kind of like a big box, which lies on your desk or stands next to your desk. I had a secretary once that would only do the latter, no matter how I begged…but that's another story. The system unit may or may not come with a disk drive, a hard drive, or instructions printed in English. It just depends on what you asked for, and whether anyone in the warehouse is smart enough to give you what you asked for.

Hard Drives and Disk Drives

Computers can't do anything without data. Data is the facts and figures you put into the computer, and then have one heck of a time getting back from the computer thirty minutes later.

On a PC, data can hide almost anywhere. Sometimes it even sneaks out the back while you're not looking. But most of the time it's either on a hard drive or a disk drive. The hard drive is a flat cylinder that spins around inside the PC. It's a good idea because it can hold a lot of data, except that the data gets really dizzy.

The disk drive is a slot in front of the PC in which you insert little disks, which also used to be called "floppies." Floppy disks used to be 5.25 inches. Now most disks are 3.5 inches. This means you'll probably have the wrong size at least half the time. I once got fed-up and tried to use a 5.25" in a 3.5", after folding it a few times. Funny thing—getting it in was not a problem. Getting it out was.

☺

The Printer

Printers today are pretty advanced...you'd be amazed at the intricate stuff that can come out of printer. In fact, you'd be amazed if any stuff at all comes out of a printer, because they usually have one heck of a time interfacing with your computer.

Either the computer's not talking or the printer's not listening, but the good news is: if you're having trouble like everyone else, at least you're saving a bundle on computer paper.

Computer Paper

Folks with fancy laser printers have no fear of computer paper. But the rest of us must cope with those scary strips of little computer paper holes, which rarely tear on the perforations...especially while the boss is waiting in your office for the printout.

Of course, computer paper holes are kid stuff when compared to the suffering caused by page alignment: the art of getting the print to start at the top of the page. While there's no reason to be afraid of computers, there's every reason to be afraid of page alignment, and many good computer careers have been ruined because of it.

Modems

Just a short word here about modems. If you have a computer at home, and you want to link to other computers, you need a modem. A modem ties up your telephone line, but you can then talk to other computers and they can talk to you.

So if someone's trying to reach you, and your line is busy for hours at a time, they'll probably assume it's because you have a modem...or maybe a teenage daughter.

The Mouse

Full-grown adults, even after hours of care and counseling, still express trepidation about getting near a keyboard. That's why someone invented the mouse. I personally don't think a mouse looks like a mouse nor sounds like a mouse, and my 2-year old daughter tells me it doesn't even taste like a mouse. The sad thing is I believe her...she's put more things in her mouth than I'd care to mention.

But a mouse rolls around on any flat surface, and lets you point to and select stuff on your screen. It's so easy to use, all it takes is one hand. This means you can use your other hand to do other important stuff...like keeping your 2-year old from sucking on the mouse.

The Other Stuff In And Around The Computer

There's a whole bunch of other hardware I'm not going to cover...which will make it a lot easier to write another book. But inside the computer there are chips, and motherboards, and switches, and all sorts of neat equipment. Take my advice: don't go near it. Stay away. You can do a heck of a lot of damage to a $3000 system with a 79 cent screwdriver.

I should also warn you about cables. Don't touch the cables. Once in a while, they get downright mean. Once you unplug them from where they were plugged, they make sure you'll never remember where they were plugged-in in the first place. I swear, it's safer just to take a scissors and cut 'em somewhere in the middle, then splice the ends back together when you're ready to get back to work.

Software

I'm always suspicious about software. You can't see it. You can't touch it. People will tell you it's on one of those 3.5" disks; I guess you have to believe them.

You can't run a computer without software, it's the stuff that tells the data what to do. So if you're bound and determined to do something with your computer, at some point you'd better go see about getting some software. But I'll warn you, it's hard to figure out, and you have to work on it for a long time before anything happens…just like most of my dates back in high-school.

Manuals

Like it or not, most hardware and software purchases come with manuals. If the stuff is expensive, then the manuals are called "documentation." If your receipt is around five bucks, then the manuals are called "instructions."

Either way, don't open them. Don't browse through the "Quick Reference." Don't leaf through the "Common Errors and Messages." No one who reads these manuals understands them. Heck, no one who *writes* these manuals understands them.

Instead, we computer professionals are bound by tradition to figure out stuff for ourselves…it's kind of our "unwritten code." That's because most of the code we need is still unwritten.

The Stuff That's Even Smaller Than PC's

Even after reading all this, if you still want to be scared, it's okay to be scared of really small computers, like notebooks and laptops. Even though they're small, they're incredibly powerful, and that's scary. And one guideline I try to follow is never put anything really scary on your lap…there's too many vulnerable body parts near there.

Even smaller that notebooks are these clever little hand-held devices. You can even buy ones now that don't even use keyboards at all, you write on them! Trust me, this is a really bad idea. When I use a computer, I always use a keyboard…it's the only reliable way to gte tihngs done.

The Stuff That's A Lot Bigger Than PC's

Finally, you can't forget about all that big hardware…the mainframes and midranges and tape drives and networks that businesses use every day to stay in business.

Some of these babies cost millions of dollars. Some need huge amounts of air-conditioning and electricity. Some require armies of highly-skilled operators. Most of them still break down six times a day (the computers, not the operators…unless it's been a long week).

Trying to figure out big hardware is half the reason why there's such a huge market for little hardware, especially beepers. But in an annual poll, CEO's have voted mainframe computers the best investment they've ever made four years running. It's when they're *not* running that these folks get a little touchy about the subject.

FOUR

The Scary People That Understand Computers

Computers aren't really the problem; some don't even look that scary. Many PC's blend well with your office decor, and most keep relatively quiet, unless they're beeping like crazy because you've made some horrible error, or left a bologna sandwich leaning on the ENTER key.

It's the people who use the computers who screw everything up. They think they're much too clever. They're way too productive. They certainly don't watch enough TV. And lots of them don't shower half as much as we'd like them to.

But instead of being scared of the people who use computers, you just need to formulate a computer-people strategy. You can join them, which is probably a bad idea unless you've already got all the proper attire. Or perhaps you can learn to live with them, learn how to avoid them, or learn how to make fun of them, which is generally the most popular option.

Whatever the case, you first have to learn how to recognize these guys. Pay attention, so you can pick them out at a distance, before they get too close and start rambling about all this floppy-mousey-RAMmy stuff.

The Computer Salesman

People have a natural fear of salesmen, and instinctively steer clear of anyone wearing a suit two sizes too small. By and large this is a good thing, because it has helped human beings survive over the centuries, especially preventing lots of them from being killed by their wives for bringing home a $4000 riding lawnmower.

But computer salesmen (and saleswomen) didn't used to be slimy. In fact, computer salesmen used to be affluent and relaxed, and you practically couldn't tell them apart from normal people. Back in those days, people actually were clamoring to buy computers of all sizes, and salesmen took orders like a pancake house waitress on Sunday morning.

But today, computers sell no more. Folks who never had one know they never will, and folks who already have one wish they never did. Prices have nose-dived. Competition is cut-throat. It's getting so a computer salesman can barely afford a decent European automobile.

That's why salesmen have rapidly become hungrier, a little pushier, and a lot slimier. They're starting to say really scary things, like, "Sure, the keyboard's missing a few letters…but at least they're not vowels, and it's a heck of a buy."

So stay away from computer salesmen. Granted, it's not like they've replaced lawyers on the list of "Most-Unwanted," but they're giving politicians and dentists a run for their money.

The Hacker

Here's someone to be very afraid of. You've got to first realize that hackers do nothing except play with computers. They eat with computers. They sleep with computers. They think, read, and dream about computers. They have no interest in the weekend pursuits of us "normal" people, like cleaning the garage or putting up storm windows. Stay away from someone who has never put up a storm window.

And then you've got to realize that some hackers are lawbreakers, even felons! They may look harmless. They may appear intelligent, gentle, and polite.

But underneath that innocent demeanor lies someone who has spent years manipulating funds, destroying valuable information, and jeopardizing the financial well-being of our nation. So if you run into someone like this, avoid them at all costs. They might be one of these keyboard criminals…or just another Executive from a Savings and Loan.

The Computer Professional

Computers are tough enough to use at home. But believe it or not, people actually use computers at work…or at least try to. Some folks get paid to implement computer technology which controls costs, streamlines processes, and provides industry-wide competitive advantage. Other folks get paid to scratch their heads and wonder why the computer's been down since Tuesday.

The trouble is, it's tough telling one Computer Professional apart from another. Some are called Analysts. Some are called Programmers. Regular folks quickly get lost trying to figure out who's who.

So, to simplify things, I've listed the ten most common jobs in Data Processing. During his or her career, an experienced Computer Professional holds four or five of these positions…and usually all at the same time.

1. PROGRAMMER. This is the lowest life form in Data Processing. Manages no one. Answers to everyone. Fifty percent of his time is spent in meetings. Fifty percent is spent writing documentation. Another fifty percent is spent filling out time cards and status reports. Any time left over is for classes on stuff he'll never use.

The Programmer is evaluated on his computer programs…never has time to write any. Hopes someday he'll be promoted to Analyst.

2. ANALYST. The Analyst refuses to write programs. Her job is to design new systems, write workflows for new systems, and devise procedures for new systems. But she'll always end-up having to train users on how to get by with the old systems. Next in line to be Team Leader.

3. TEAM LEADER. Team Leaders manage one project. They don't know why they're not called Project Leaders; they have it on their resumes.

4. PROJECT LEADER. Manages several projects at once. Analyzes reports from the Team Leaders' projects. Monitors schedules from the Team Leaders' projects. Has absolutely no idea what any of the projects are about. Wants to be a Programmer again.

5. OPERATOR. The Operator wields powers that the

Project Leader can only dream about. Makes Programmers beg for computer tapes. Makes Analysts beg for printout. Makes Team Leaders beg for test time. Has a true appreciation of the career potential in the computer industry…that's why he's going to Law School at night.

6. SYSTEMS PROGRAMMER. Even Operators want to be System Programmers…System Programmers have a great sense of humor. They make programs appear then disappear then re-appear again, especially when Programmers are working all night. And when the mood strikes them, they can crash the system without warning, usually while some Project Leader is giving a demo to the CEO.

7. DBA. DBA stands for Data Base Administrator. No one really knows what the DBA does, and no one is smart enough to know if the DBA is doing it. But every company must have one, because no place can afford two of them.

8. LAN ADMINISTRATOR. Watches over the company's *L*ocal *A*rea *N*etwork. Some companies have dozens of networks. Some networks have hundreds of PC's. The LAN Administrator makes sure these PC's can talk to the mainframe. The LAN Administrator makes sure these PC's can talk to the other PC's. But no one can ever talk to the LAN Administrator…she's always out fiddling with someone's PC.

9. DEPARTMENT SECRETARY. In most companies, folks have their own phonemail, E-mail, and word-processing. This leaves the Department Secretary with all kinds of time to dispense the three most basic human needs: paychecks, rumors, and supplies. Also makes the copier self-destruct just by going to lunch.

10. THE CIO. CIO stands for Chief Information Officer. CIOs want to finish next year's budget. They want to finish last year's appraisals. They want to learn the names of one or two of their Programmers. Instead, CIOs only have time to hide from Users and reschedule meetings. CIOs have managed sophisticated computer technology for years...so many years, they haven't a clue how it works anymore.

The 3rd-Grader

Children spend most of their childhood convinced they know more than you. Computers give them the chance to prove it. They use one in science class. They've seen one at Stacy's house. By the time they're ten, they can discuss databases. They can format diskettes. Somehow they can demonstrate an uncanny grasp of complex, high-tech concepts, and still forget to close the door to the fridge.

Computers just seem to be everywhere. I still remember the day my nephew came home from school and boasted,

"Right after recess, we watched Big Bird use a computer on TV!" Stuff like that really amazes me...especially since the kid is 19 and a sophomore in college.

The Public Programmer

Most people who fear computers are upset enough as it is. But what makes things worse is people who *publicly* pound-away on computers. They mostly do it on airplanes, hovering over their notebooks and laptops, trying to set-up one more spreadsheet between L.A. and El Paso.

I'm actually not adverse to computing on airplanes. First off, laptops make air-travelers look intelligent and respect-able, and for some folks that's their only hope. Second, a lap usually is a pre-requisite for a laptop, which might help set a goal for one guy who's sitting in 23E, F, *and* G.

But what's so horribly annoying about folks who compute in coach is their smug "I'm-working-on-my-career-while-you're-sitting-there-waiting-for-the-stewardess-to-bring-a-turkey-croissant" expression. So at the slightest turbulence, take my advice and innocently spill a can of Ginger Ale all over the closest available laptop (and lap). Or better yet, if you can stomach the stuff, ask for tomato juice.

The IS Entrepreneur

IS Entrepreneurs are the scariest people of all. They wouldn't be so bad if they wore ties. Or had grey hair. Or were old and fat. But these kids still get pimples. They look like the guys you used to beat up in high school. Heck, they probably are.

And now these wiz-kids, both men and women, are socking-away millions, acquiring companies, and playing frisbee at lunch.

I'm an open-minded person. I don't hold a grudge against anyone because they're smart, or successful, or so pitifully anti-social and maladjusted they spent their sorry teenage years sticking wires into a motherboard.

There's nothing bad about making millions. The big rock stars do, right? So do pro athletes. But face it, rock stars and athletes have strength and skill, or at least look great in a pair of jeans. I can handle that. But I can't handle some wimp who starts a computer company, makes millions, and still gets taped with a KICK ME sign at least once a week.

FIVE

Bad Things That Sometimes Happen

By now, perhaps you're thinking about using a computer, or at least finding out what one looks like. But think again, because some very bad things can happen to nice people who get too close to a computer.

For example, my aunt once got one leg of her pantyhose caught in a printer...it took ten minutes and twenty-two pages to get her out. No one's quite sure how it happened, and she's never much inclined to talk about it.

That's why, before jumping in with both feet and a

checkbook, you should be prepared to deal with some pretty scary stuff. Computers are not for the faint of heart. They're complex. They're frustrating. You'll often find yourself hovering over your computer for two or three hours at a time…just trying to find the on/off switch.

So if you're foolish enough to want a computer, it's best you be prepared. Monkeying with a computer is not like changing your oil or replacing the bag in a vacuum cleaner. Come to think of it, I can't remember the last time I changed the bag in my vacuum cleaner. And I probably should…I used it to change my oil.

Compatibility Problems

Computer users are constantly confronted with compatibility problems; just ask any girl they asked-out in high school. No matter how many manuals you read, no matter how much money your spend; you can still get bit by computer incompatibility.

For example, your over-priced software might not work with your current operating system. Or the expensive printer you just bought only works with the mega-expensive computer you can't afford. Or you can encounter the most common compatibility issue of all: when the box containing your new monitor won't fit in the back of your Ford Fiesta.

Printer Problems

Computers are easy, compared to printers. Just about everything goes wrong with printers, especially those cheap ones with the pinfeed wheels, ribbons, and computer paper with the little holes. You'll soon discover that the more moving parts your printer has, the greater the odds that one of them won't be moving at all.

Running out of paper is your first nightmare. Don't ever try to re-load continuous form paper into a printer. You're better off just giving up and doing something a little less painful, like having a root canal.

Changing a printer ribbon is even worse. Never do it. When your ribbon wears out, just go buy a new printer. Trust me. The only time I tried to get a ribbon *out* of a printer, the ribbon wound up in several pieces. The only time I tried to get a ribbon *into* a printer, the printer wound up in several pieces.

Software Errors

Don't get upset when your software's not working. Nothing's wrong. Software never works, or when it does, few people are smart enough to know it. In fact, if your ever think your software's working, something *really* must be wrong.

Error Messages

On the subject of software errors, the worst thing about them is the error messages. No one understands error messages. Most of them are undecipherable, and show-up as mysterious codes composed of numbers, letters, and portions of the Greek alphabet.

Why can't a computer tell you what's wrong in English? Why can't the computer just say, "Excuse me, you numbskull, but you forgot to turn on the printer"? Instead, you get this crazy error code which says, "EIE-IO: input/output device not available," and then the computer, printer, and all their chummy input and output devices laugh at you behind your back.

Troubleshooting

Most of the time, your computer won't work. Sometimes it will be because it's broken. Sometimes it will be because you *think* it's broken. That's when you have to troubleshoot: so that you can tell who is doing what they're *not* supposed to…you or the computer.

Ninety percent of the time, troubleshooting will uncover human error, and prove the computer's not broken. The rest of the time, troubleshooting will uncover human error, then break the computer. Most computer manuals describe four basic steps in the troubleshooting process:

1. Investigate the problem
2. Isolate the hardware and software symptoms
3. Determine if documentation exists on these symptoms
4. Cuss a lot, then smack the side of the computer.

There are usually three devices with which most computer novices have the most trouble troubleshooting:

1. *Monitor not working.* In the event of monitor failure, use the following five-step monitor-troubleshooting checklist. Is the monitor plugged in? Is it turned on? Is it upside down? Is it facing the right way? Are you facing the right way?

2. *Mouse not working.* First, make sure you're not using a real mouse. It happened to me once and it was most unpleasant; probably even more so for the mouse. Then, roll the mouse around. Does the cursor stay in one spot on the screen? Either the mouse is broken, or you're not looking at the cursor, but rather what's left from an old sneeze.

3. *Husband not working.* Tell him to get off that darn computer and get his butt into work.

Expert consensus, when it comes to troubleshooting, is never do it. Save yourself the frustration. Just pack up your system. Bring it down to your car. Get in your car. Then back the car over it and smash it into little pieces.

☺

Break-Downs

Even the best troubleshooters concede: computers break. Break-downs are unavoidable. Years of statistics have proven that most computers tend to break-down either:

1. at the worst conceivable moment, or

2. all the time, including the worst conceivable moment.

If you're at work, a break-down is no big deal, because companies usually pay somebody a whole bunch of money to show up three or four times before bringing the right parts to fix the computer.

But if your home computer kicks the bucket, you're in a world of hurt. Maybe you can spend eight hours and fix it. Maybe you can spend eight hours and find out you can't fix it. But usually you have to box-up the whole thing, load it into the back of your car, and take it all the way across town to someone who can't fix it.

SIX

Really Bad Things
That Always Happen

After reading the gory details of Chapter 5, few folks would still have a stomach for computers. Why would anyone want to spend so much money and be constantly frustrated and upset? It's almost as bad as golf.

But if all this stuff doesn't scare you, then it's time to drag-up the heinous and hard-core calamities of computing. Children, consult your parents before reading ahead...because some computing-events are so terrible, so painful, and so nauseating that high-tech professionals won't even talk about them, especially after dark.

The public has a right to know. But brace yourself for the worst things that happen when you use a computer. Fortunately, statistics show that only one of these things will ever happen to you. Unfortunately, it will probably happen two or three times a day.

Bugs

Bugs are pretty scary. Bugs happen when your computer won't do what it's supposed to.

Most of us need not worry about bugs, since we have no idea what computers are supposed to do in the first place. But once you get the hang of a computer, a bug can sneak-up out of nowhere and kill the better part of an hour, a day, or a career.

Bugs come in all sizes. Little bugs convince your computer to print words like "Pennsyltucky," then make all

your sub-totals appear in Hebrew. Bigger bugs cause your computer to "crash," which means everything stops, weird messages fill the screen, and you then phone your husband to say you'll be late for dinner.

You can't actually *see* a bug, but it's easy to tell when someone's got one. If you're minding your own business when you hear the sound of a keyboard hitting a wall, odds are the guy in the next office ran into a bug.

Viruses

Bugs are bad, but viruses are worse. Bugs are usually an accident…a software mistake caused by someone working much too late, or carelessly writing a program while watching "Oprah." But viruses are deliberate. Someone is trying to mess up your computer by locking your keyboard, wiping out your data, or unleashing a little PacMan that eats-up all your W's.

And viruses can spread…into other PC's, into larger computers, even into adjacent appliances. A really mean virus can destroy your hard drive, and simultaneously make the microwave overzap your Lean Cuisine by a good minute-and-a-half.

The world is poorly-prepared for viruses, unable to curb the spread of technically-transmitted diseases. Short of diskette-condoms, the best you can do is hope your computer doesn't interface with other computers, or at least won't stay out late on a school night.

If you suspect you have a virus, don't take chances. Don't mess with anti-virus software. Don't procrastinate. You need to swiftly, but humanely, put your computer to death. At the first virus-like symptom, unplug the whole system and pitch it over the cubicle wall. This may seem a little drastic, and there's a slight chance you'll accidently hit a nearby Computer Professional. But if you're lucky, maybe you'll hit two of them.

Dirty screens

Dirty computer screens are much more dangerous than you think. Never touch the screen. It's not a question of low-level radiation, or static electricity, or electro-magnetic fields.

It's a question of whether your office manager spots you laying a greasy fingerprint on your screen, and whether she can hit the back of your head with a can of aerosol cleaner, even from all the way across the room.

Losing support

You can do all kinds of research. You can talk to all kinds

of salespeople. You can wind up with the perfect computer that fits your budget, makes it home in one piece, and eventually does computer stuff within the first twenty or thirty times you try to get it to do computer stuff.

But out of nowhere, something terrible can happen: you can lose support. The company that made it doesn't work on it any more. They don't stock the parts. They don't fix the software. If you're "down," you're down for good. To put it in the proper high-tech terminology: you've been screwed.

Hardware and software come and go; loss-of-support can happen to anybody. Don't take it personally. Don't immediately go into therapy, or consume large quantities of Fudge Ripple ice cream. These days, new computers become obsolete in the time it takes to drop off your dry-cleaning. So accept loss-of-support as a way of life. Simply put: Technology waits for no man...although I'd bet it's waited a time or two for a woman to get dressed to go out for dinner.

Hotlines

Once in a great while, your hardware will work properly while your software is having a rough day. Or maybe your software is working fine, but your printer has a touch of indigestion. This is when you must confront the most revolting and traumatic experience in high-tech: the Hotline.

Most computer companies try to provide a hotline. Usually, when their stuff's not working, their hotline's not either. But in everyone's life, *one* of three events will happen: you will win the lottery, you will get struck by lightning, or you will get through to someone working at the Hotline.

A truly experienced customer can be trained to navigate through the maze of automated operators and bad hold-music, eventually reaching one or two of the real human beings working the hotline, and usually within the time it takes to play a full NBA season.

Hotlines actually fill a major void in the computer industry. If there is a population of customers who enjoy being told they are total idiots, a hotline comes in handy. For those lonely folks who have nothing to do between New Year's and Easter, "hotline holding" is an inexpensive way to pass the time. And finally, there's that high-tech career path that only the Hotline can provide...for those who aspire, someday, to be the next available representative.

Losing Everything

Losing everything is the most gruesome occurence in high-tech, not including the Hotline. Losing everything happens when all the stuff you and your computer have been working on for the last three years suddenly disappears.

Maybe your hard drive becomes violently sick. Maybe your daughter crams a PopTart in your disk drive. Whatever the case, you're *supposed* to back everything up to diskette once in a while.

But while your dog is consuming a box of diskettes because to him they look (and probably taste) like Wendy's hamburger patties, the mutt usually won't have the courtesy to spare the backup diskettes. So be smart. Find a high shelf somewhere; someplace that practically no one can reach...then stick your dog up there.

Granted, losing everything may seem pretty scary, but don't be all that terrified. Losing everything only happens once in your computer lifetime. Because, after that, you're sure never to touch a blasted computer again.

SEVEN

Hiding From Computers

I'm not going to frantically wave my arms and tell you computers are great and everyone has to have one. The last time I tried it was not very pleasant, especially since my wife smacked me several times with a dirty spatula while I tried to sneak in the house with $6000 worth of equipment.

So if you want to forever avoid computers, I won't stand in your way. But I feel obligated to tell you…it won't be easy.

Think about it. You rent a car. You buy a Big Mac. You wait in the 10-items-or-less line for an hour or so. In each case, you're surrounded by computers.

Of course, *you* don't have to use them. Some high-school kid's getting minimum wage to scan a cans of peas. Some sophomore is punching in your order for extra pickles. But Lord forbid you fork over a ten dollar bill just before the power goes out...the kid will become paralyzed, unable to even venture a guess at the change on a $9.50 purchase.

Computers are everywhere. But the tricky part is: lots of them don't even look like computers. They're well hidden. They're impossible to avoid. Just when you think it's safe, you'll walk into a computer that's reading in, printing out, counting up, or breaking down.

ATM's

Years ago, banker's hours meant locking the door at 3:00, then spending hours balancing drawers by hand. Today, financial systems move funds in the blink of an eye. Computers balance a million accounts in seconds. You can't help but marvel at the power of all this technology, especially while you're standing in line behind someone depositing $65.00 in pennies.

But where computers are even more evident are in the ATM—the Automatic Teller Machine. The ATM started out as a good idea. It's nice to be able to get at your money 24 hours a day…except for folks with an ex-wife or two. But as popular as ATM's are today, when they first came out, no one used them. That's because either everyone was afraid of the computer in the ATM, or because no one had any money in the first place.

You can hide from ATM's; you don't have to use them. But they're really not that spooky. Once you get your card right side up, the computer asks some pretty simple questions, and you're on your way. Using an ATM should be an easy and quick process. Yet somehow it never is for the two idiots in front of you, especially when it's raining and you forgot your coat.

The Telephone

You know you can't hide from the telephone. Believe me, I've tried, but my mother-in-law still gets through every Sunday.

There are all kinds of fancy phones that actually contain computers. But did you know the entire telephone network is full of computers? You'd be amazed at all the technology that goes into the phone system, even though an operator can't tell when you've lost a quarter in a pay phone.

But you don't need to hide from computerized telephone systems, you need to hide from computerized *answering* systems. Long gone are the days when someone used to answer the phone. Now you're answered by a compu-voice, who asks you to press 1 if you want to check your balance, or press 2 if you forgot what would happen if your pressed 1, or press "*" if you're calling from a rotary dial phone.

I've never been too happy about compu-voice systems; none are much faster than the US Mail. Although I did once date the girl whose voice was used for all those compu-voice messages. All told, we had a pretty good time, until I reached for the wrong button and she gave me the pound sign.

Cash Registers

When was the last time you heard a cash register go "ka-ching"? No one ka-chings anymore. Everyone uses these fancy compu-registers that beep and blink and print out little computer receipts.

Maybe compu-registers were invented to improve my life, but I know it's made the cashier's life a living hell. She needs 10 minutes to change the compu-register paper. She takes 20 minutes to return the sweater Aunt Sylvia gave me for Christmas…it probably didn't even take that long to make it. And you'd better hope she never thinks the 33%-off socks are the 25%-off socks, lest she need to summon her supervisor, the store owner, and a programmer from New Jersey just to void the last entry.

Computers Around Your Home

Don't look now, but you're surrounded. Remember the VCR in the den? It's hiding a computer. Of course, how smart can this computer be if every time I try to tape the Vikings game I wind up with the Weather Channel? I can't imagine why anyone would tape the Weather Channel...although if anyone wants to know the weather the past few Sundays, give me a call.

And what about all the other computers hidden in your house? Your alarm clock? Microwave oven? Home security system? Toilet? You probably don't buy the one about the toilet. But mine has a computer in it...my kid flushed my pocket calculator.

Your Car

The automotive industry is certainly not avoiding computers. Cars and trucks are full of them. There're computerized sensors, monitors, controls and gadgets under the hood and around the dash. They've made cars more reliable, fuel efficient, and safe. Well, maybe not safe. My neighbor once got stopped by a cop because his car was full of computers...he'd just stolen twenty of them from an appliance store.

With all these computers in cars, you can't afford to be afraid. Where are you going to hide? In the back seat? The trunk? Might only work if you were going to a Drive-In movie. And there're even computers in gas pumps, in tune-up shops, even in toll booths. There're so many cars with computers on the road today, you can't help but run into one everywhere you go. At least that's the excuse my wife uses.

Your Body

This gets pretty scary, because hiding from your body doesn't sound too easy. You're pretty well stuck with yourself, whether you like it or not, except maybe for the stuff you don't want to lose, like hair or cleavage.

But someday, if not today, you may be filled with electronics…you may become a walking computer. Think about folks with pacemakers, or the latest hearing aids. Or what about headphones, or your Walkman? Maybe they're the reason you need a hearing aid.

Think about your watch! Some are loaded with computers. Mine even has a little Mickey Mouse sitting at a keyboard. And what computerized sneakers? I think there is such a thing...or at least the sneakers cost like they had computers.

Tomorrow, computers will be everywhere...around you, next to you; even inside you! It's a frightening thought. It may be a little hard to swallow. But with the tiny size of computers today, I wouldn't be surprised if I've swallowed a few already.

EIGHT

Taking The First Step

If you are brave enough to be reading this chapter, perhaps you are now ready to work with a computer. This is a very important milestone in your life, and like a wedding or the birth of a child, it's something that should be given careful thought.

That's not to even remotely imply you should shy away from life's major commitments. Millions of people have spouses, children, or computers…sometimes lots of each. But I am convinced the combination of all three spells nothing but trouble. That's why I'm giving you one last chance to turn back. For the curious and strong, let's move ahead.

The key to a successful and sane computer experience is accepting the two basic principles of the human-computer relationship:

1. No human is smarter than a computer, not even a PC. Personal Computers have superior memory, power, and logic, and can make humans feel weak and insignificant by comparison.

2. A human can always push a PC off a table.

Now that you know your place in respect to technology, let's get started with computers.

Buying A Computer

If you're using a computer at work, you'll never have to worry about buying a new computer. You'll never even have to worry about *getting* a new computer. That's because it's the *other* people at work who get the new computer, while folks like you always wind-up getting their *old* computer. Don't lose too much sleep over this blatant corporate injustice: new computers aren't any easier to figure out than old computers.

But if you want a new computer for your home, you have a lot of options. You can go to a retail store and pay top dollar, you can go to a garage sale and get a bargain computer that looks pretty good, given that a couple of sides are held together with masking tape, or you can do several things in between.

1. Computer stores. If you're new, start at a computer store. There's nothing wrong with needing lots of help, asking a lot of questions, learning about all the features and options, and spending three times as much as you planned in the first place. Sure, you may feel vulnerable and embarassed not knowing a thing about computers…but odds are the salesman doesn't, either.

The good thing about a computer store is the reliability and service. You can always go back to ask questions. You can always go back if a part is defective. You can always go back if you can't figure out what you're doing. But if you go back four or five times on the first day, and are pounding on the glass at closing time…maybe you need some extra help.

2. Extra help. There are consultants who, for a small fee, will come to your house, recommend a solution, get you the best price, set the system up, and even teach you how to use it. This service is worth every penny. There's no telling how much frustration and suffering you avoid by having a system that's up and running…at least until minutes after the consultant has backed his car out of your driveway.

3. Catalogs. Believe it or not, you can even order computers through the mail, at a great discount price. The novice, however, should be a little careful about mail-order; it's sometimes hard to tell what you're getting (or not getting!) just by reading a catalog. Take your time, call for help, and make sure you're getting the right computer. Because when your box arrives, and it sounds like it contains a jigsaw puzzle, you probably didn't get the right computer.

4. Appliance stores. Computer stores aren't the only places that sell computers. Appliance stores, department stores and discount stores carry them. Of course, some of the guys carrying them also drop them when nobody's looking.

You've got to make your own decision on appliance stores. Do you want to buy a computer from a guy who also sells washers and car stereos? Odds are you'll find a computer at a very low price. But you may also find a computer with a permanent press setting…at least your data won't wrinkle.

5. Used computers. If you want to buy a used computer, it's always pretty easy. Of course, if you want to *sell* a used computer, it's always darn near impossible.

But every newspaper and electronic bulletin board advertises dozens of used computers. Be cautious. You never know what's really inside. You never know what you're getting. But since most of us have absolutely no idea what we're getting anyway, a used computer might not be a bad idea.

6. Building your own computer. You've got to be extremely patient, intelligent, or bored to try this. You have to have a detailed knowledge of electronics, you have to go buy all the little parts, and you also have to hope none of them roll off the table and down a floor vent. No matter what I build, a crucial piece always seems to roll off the table and down a floor vent...a fact I usually discover about ten minutes after I *think* I'm done.

Anyway, when you build a computer yourself, you can always be sure of the quality...which is generally pretty lousy. Granted, in the seventies a couple of guys tried this and got rich and famous. But in the nineties, all you're likely to get is a frying pan over your head for spending too much time in the basement while your wife has to watch the kids.

Software

Hold it, you're not done! The hardware is the easy part...you now have to buy the software, or at least copy it from your neighbor.

Of course, you're not really allowed to copy software, it's against the law. Don't do it, or soon you'll sink deeper into a life of crime, eventually going so far as to rip tags off mattresses or use the pictures, accounts and descriptions of a Major League Baseball game without anyone's expressed written consent.

What you may find somewhat upsetting is that, compared

to software, hardware is *easy*. You're going to need operating system software, applications software, spreadsheet software, database software…you could get a hernia just getting the stuff to the car. But you've got to have software; it's what tells everything what to do…kind of the high-tech equivalent of in-laws.

Where To Put A Computer

The best place for a computer is on your desk…*at work*. Don't bring a computer into your house. But if you're determined to be just as miserable in both places, you'll need to find the right spot for your home computer.

1. Not the kitchen. A computer is not for recipes and shopping lists. Do not cover it with little magnets in the shape of carrots or corn-on-the-cob. You'll find that putting a computer in a cool, clean, and safe spot really extends the life of your computer. Dousing the keyboard with marinara sauce *doesn't*.

2. Not the den. A computer won't last fifteen minutes in the den. The kids will immediately start using it for games, and while some computers handle games pretty well, one good round of computer baseball can ruin a computer, especially when the computer *is* the baseball.

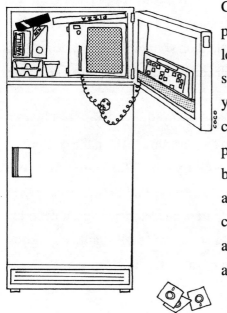

3. Not the bedroom. Computers have wrecked plenty of marriages, or at least made lots of guys sleep on the couch. If you're already fairly insecure about what you do, or perhaps don't do in the bedroom, it's probably not a good place for a computer…even a laptop at the wrong time can really kill the mood.

4. Not the home office. Folks who are lucky enough to have an office at home think this is the perfect place for a computer. This is not the case. Granted, given the right environment, light, and humidity, a computer in a home office can last longer than a color TV. But if you're smart, you'll just forget the whole thing and go watch the color TV.

Computer Furniture

At this point, you may want to place your new computer

on some very nice, expensive computer furniture. Of course, not all computers need expensive computer furniture. It's a bad idea for a two-ton water-cooled mainframe. And a laptop doesn't need furniture...put it on your lap! Or try putting it on someone else's lap, which can be a lot of fun, or make a date end somewhat abruptly.

Lots of places sell computer furniture. Try to follow one rule: don't spend more on the furniture than on the computer. You may be tempted to try do-it-yourself furniture, like an old folding card table, barstool, and a hula-lamp from your trip to Hawaii. Don't do it. Computers need something stable; odds are good a computer can fall off a card table...although not as many times as I've fallen off a barstool.

Setting Up A Computer

Find a big, flat, clean surface, and open all the boxes. But don't rip the boxes! You'll need them to transport your computer when it breaks, which statistics show will happen right after you've spent all night trying to put the thing together, or right after your warranty has expired...whichever comes first.

Take everything out of every box, and lay it carefully on the floor. At this point, you will see that you have a couple sets of instructions, a whole mess of styrofoam, and a bunch of other stuff which (hopefully) will eventually look like a computer.

Next, make sure everything is right side up. That's harder than it sounds, except for maybe the keyboard. Now, start stacking components on top of each other until anything looks anything like any of the pictures on any of the boxes. This may take a while.

Once accomplished, connect the cables. This is the really hard part. Cables have these weird clips and plugs at each end, with a configuration of "pins" that match holes in the computer. The challenge is to match the right end of the right cable with the right hole in the computer, before you go right out of your mind. Randomly select a cable and a hole, and give it a try. After six or seven forceful attempts, step back and maybe try a running start. If it still won't connect, try another cable, or better yet, try another hobby besides computers.

If you think you're done and there's nothing left dangling, plug it in and power it on! Don't be afraid of electrocuting yourself…you should be happy you've gotten this far without serious injury. In fact, there's only one documented case of computer electrocution, and that was someone who assembled his computer on the flat, big, clean surface of his shower floor.

☺

Figuring Out How To Use A Computer

This part of the computer experience takes the longest, except maybe for the time it takes to get the purchase completely off your credit card.

Most students of computers begin with TAE. TAE starts as "Trial And Error," which soon gives way to "Terror And Error," which eventually becomes "Throw Away Everything." But there are alternatives, most of which, by comparison, are just as frustrating and painful.

You can buy computer books. Computer books are a cheap, private way to teach yourself computers at your own pace. Just make sure your own pace does not require making any noticeable progress for a decade or so.

You can also take a class. You can find classes at your computer store, local high school or community college. Classes are time-consuming, expensive, and frustrating, but at least you can meet a lot of people who share your predicament... and one of them might buy your computer so you can forget the whole thing.

NINE

Regretting The First Step

By now it's too late. You have probably become a computer user and there's no turning back. You've traded your computer virginity for night after endless night of debugging, designing, and similar high-tech debauchery.

Of course, you may experience a few months of denial and depression. Or you may wonder why all this is happening to you. There is nothing to be ashamed of. Thousands of people use computers, but otherwise lead normal and somewhat painless lives.

So if folks stare at you on the subway, or talk about you after you get off the elevator, it's probably got nothing to do with computers, and a lot to do with what you spilled on your tie at lunch. Be proud of your new computer heritage. Come out of the closet, make the best of it, and start doing the scary stuff that other computer people do.

Use Acronyms

Do this ASAP. Abbreviate everything. Computer people are supposed to impress non-computer people with endless initials and boatloads of buzzwords.

To start with, there's too many long words in high-tech. You can't say mega-phrases like "Distributed Computing Environment Protocols" twenty times in a meeting. Everyone would get really frustrated, especially the next group waiting to use the conference room.

So people just abbreviate, and soon no one has the foggiest idea what the acronym stands for in the first place…which is no big deal, since no one has the foggiest idea what Distributed Computing Environment Protocols are supposed to do, anyway.

Wear Computer Clothes

You used to have to wear computer clothes. Computer people customarily donned white socks, thick glasses, short pants, and pocket protectors…and that was just the women.

Today, computer users wear whatever they want. Some dress like punk rockers. Some dress like housewives. Some dress in three piece suits, except the three pieces are rarely from the same suit. High-tech and high-fashion hardly ever cross paths; it's the computer professionals that keep the demand for polyester at a feverish peak.

Read Computer Literature

Do you enjoy *Fortune? Time? People?* Cancel your subscriptions. Yank them off your coffee tables and out of your bathrooms. Computer folks have to read mainframe magazines and PC publications…it's some kind of masochistic requirement. No more *Sports Illustrated*. No more *Cosmopolitan*. Just computer literature, and maybe an occasional *MAD* Magazine.

High-tech reading prevents you from becoming technically stale. You need to read every techno-rag you can get your hands on. Enjoying it is another story. Humans have an instinctive aversion to 18-page articles entitled, "Fun with Fonts" or "Getting to Know your Hard Drive."

There's only one thing worse than sitting on a plane next to some goofball reading "Getting to Know your Hard Drive"…and that's listening to him talk about it all the way to Phoenix.

☺

Sign-On To Bulletin Boards

There is truly a subculture of Bulletin Board users in high-tech. A computer Bulletin Board is just what it sounds like, except it's on line, about 10,000 very weird people are reading or posting messages to it, and 90% of the network traffic is stuff you'd never want your mother to see.

There are lots of juicy, X-rated Bulletin Boards. There are also plenty of legitimate, boring Bulletin Boards: for buying and selling equipment, for tips on hardware and software, and for instructions on how to get into all the X-rated Bulletin Boards.

There's nothing wrong with Bulletin Boards. There are probably only a few that are explicit or politically extreme. But be prepared when you sign-on to any Bulletin Board, especially at night. You can get some pretty strange and shocking messages…but none more shocking than where your wife says she'll stick that computer if you don't turn it off and get to bed.

☺

User Groups and Conferences

Not only do you have to put up with computers, you now have to put up with the people who use them. You can join a User Group, which is a "club" of folks that use similar hardware, software, or printer ribbons.

User groups are an important way to load-up on new tips and techniques, information, and cheap onion dip. They're also a good way to meet people and make new friends. For computer users this is very important, because your old friends won't get near you, except maybe with a sharp stick.

Computer conferences are large gatherings of high-tech enthusiasts. These often take place in big hotels and convention centers, attracting compu-folks from all over the country. But why would anyone in their right mind would want to get thousands of compulsive computer jocks together in one place? Probably so the rest of us can enjoy a day or two of peace and quiet.

Computers At Work

If you're going to go through all the anguish of using a computer, you may as well use one at work. This might be your shortcut up the company ladder. Show-up in the office with spreadsheets, graphs, and four-color pie charts. It's a great way to amaze your boss, impress Executives, and tick off everyone else in the department.

Of course, lots of office folks now have computers on and around their desks. These guys are selfishly after your high-tech limelight. The competition is fierce...there's a massive effort afoot to establish computer superiority.

You and your co-workers can go crazy trying to out-wit and out-print the other. This can turn a once productive office into a high-tech hell, especially when everyone discovers that upper management gave the promotion to a guy who can't even use an electric pencil sharpener, but was smart enough to date the boss's daughter.

Computer Paraphenalia

Computer paraphenalia includes all the rest of the stuff that makes you an official and easily-recognized computer user. You've got the old stand-by's, like Far Side calendars, Murphy's Law posters, and cartons of Camels. Then there's the standard collection of mugs, paperweights, and pens.

But computing is not a life-style, it's a culture. You've got to be surrounded by computer by-products twenty-four hours a day. Those little computer paper hole strips have to be tumbling out of every home wastebasket. Stacks of old 5 1/4" floppies must be crammed under coffee tables to keep them from wobbling. And you can't forget that "Beam me up,

Scotty" bumper-sticker, the universally-accepted symbol of computer commuters.

Look, there's nothing terrible, intimidating, or dangerous about all this computer stuff. The computer culture is comparatively harmless...they don't solicit at airports, wear leather, or pick fights in bars. Granted, some computer users might tend to get a touchy on occasion, and try to electronically destroy entire corporations, or maybe just a couple of government agencies. But they always seem so quiet and polite about it...you really can't get too upset.

TEN

Mastering Your Computer

At this point, you might think you're pretty handy with a computer. I'm not about to argue with you, but there's a big difference between *being* pretty handy and *thinking* you're pretty handy.

For example, I used to think I was pretty handy at carving the traditional Thanksgiving bird, until the year I took few slices out of my uncle's tie. It really wasn't my fault...he always sits right next to the turkey, and wears that stupid bow tie. I guess he was pretty upset, since he immediately hurled a pan of Aunt Ida's broccoli soufflé in my general direction, and that's got to weigh at least fifteen pounds.

But back to computers, it may indeed be that you're pretty handy and are dabbling in databases, pounding out programs, and feeling somewhat computer competent. Maybe you're even hanging out in bars, hassling tough-guys about who's got the faster microchip.

But be warned: only a handful of folks ever truly master their computer. And those who do are in search of the ultimate satisfaction of living in harmony with high-tech...either that, or they're trying to make a quick buck.

Wherever you are in the spectrum, if you want to show your computer who's boss, there are lots of ways to do it. If you've really mastered your computer, then you should be able to handle things like:

The Electronic Highway

Heavyweights use the Electronic Highway as a window to the world. With the Electronic Highway, you can do your banking using your home computer. You can pay your bills. You can pay my bills; I'm not proud. You can even buy and sell stock, make airline reservations, or check the weather in Boise.

Using the Electronic Highway is not that complicated,

once you get the hang of it. It's also a great way to save time and money. And saving money is almost as good as making money…at least that's what my wife says when there's a One-Day Sale at the mall.

Taxes By Computer

I hate doing taxes. Government comes up with several really bad ideas every century or so, and taxes rank right up there with left turns during rush hour. Most people just can't take the hassle and pay someone else to do their taxes. I will too, as soon as my accountant gets back from prison.

But I understand you can now do your taxes by computer, and even submit them electronically. High-tech skills like these are a pretty good sign that you've mastered your computer. To use tax software, you either have to be very smart, or at least have a computer that's very smart…one that automatically sifts through a shoe box and tells the difference between receipts, pay stubs, old socks, and two-for-one pizza coupons.

Consulting and Computer Services

Now let's talk about making some real money. If you can do your own taxes by computer, why not do other folks' taxes?

Taxes are a great way to get into the computer services industry. But make sure you know what you're doing. There's an old saying: a quick way to lose a friend is to do their taxes. But a quicker way to lose a friend is to lose their taxes somewhere in your computer.

Even better than computer services is consulting. In consulting, you don't have to do anything, you just tell other people how to do stuff. Recommend computer solutions. Suggest systems designs. Of course, computers can make or break a business, so get a little practice before you jump into the field. Consulting for a big, powerful company can be awfully dangerous, especially when they suddenly become a small, not-so-powerful company because of you.

Writing Software

Software is where the big money is. So find a product or service with huge demand (fast-food, pizza delivery, *Sports Illustrated* swimsuit issues, etc.) and write some software for it. Don't spend a lot of time on software for just one or two users! Software to manage your cousin's moth collection may earn his eternal gratitude, but one good McSoftware program can set you up for life.

An even bigger killing awaits the authors of game software. Kids and adults can't spend their money fast enough...the market's been skyrocketing since 1980, and Nintendo is now practically a household word. At least it is in my household, where you can frequently hear such reassuring childhood merriment coming from the den, like, "Give me the controls to Nintendo, dear brother, or I will bash your head in."

Never under-estimate the power of video games. During the early eighties, most people recognized "Ms. PacMan," but couldn't identify the president who preceded Reagan. So write some video game software, and retire young. Even the guy who invented PONG was a millionaire before 40…except he went crazy, claiming he couldn't get that stupid beeping noise out of his head.

Computing For A Living

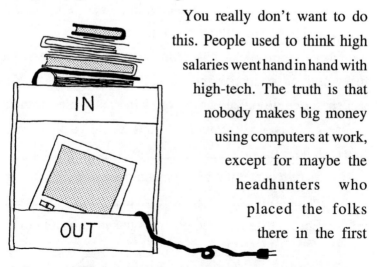

You really don't want to do this. People used to think high salaries went hand in hand with high-tech. The truth is that nobody makes big money using computers at work, except for maybe the headhunters who placed the folks there in the first

Computers are just way too complicated for anyone to try to use at work. Mastering them is downright impossible, and you can spend years of frustration and disappointment just trying to log on.

So if you're bound and determined to compute for a living, remember this: millions of people have spent their entire lives trying to build systems that make their employer more efficient. Sadly, of all these poor souls, only a handful have succeeded. Even worse, they all worked for the IRS.

Telecommuting

Finally, if you indeed have mastered your computer at work, then you can reach the pinnacle of computer competence by mastering your computer at work while you are really at home. This is called "telecommuting," which means you get paid to hang around the house in your pajamas.

Of course, in order to telecommute, your boss will demand that you are as productive and miserable as everyone else. You can't be too comfortable, or everyone will want to telecommute, and several major societal institutions would go all to heck, like rush hour traffic.

So make your home environment as bad as your work environment. Buy lots of junk food and vending machine coffee. Ensure that the temperature is unbearably cold in the winter, and even colder in the summer. Get a copier that's always broken, call lots of boring meetings with yourself, and buy cheap toilet paper for your bathroom and run out of it as often as possible.

Telecommuting will never really catch on. As an industrial nation, we simply have invested too much in the research and development of car phones, polyester ties, three-martini lunches and company cafeterias. But while the fad lasts, it would be a good idea if everyone tried it...especially everyone that's in front of me on the ramp to I-75.

ELEVEN

Kicking The Habit

So you're no longer scared of computers. That, in itself, should scare the heck out of you. You are now what you've tried to avoid all your life…it's like becoming a parent.

Computers will change your life. They will soon eat-up most of your time, thought, and effort. In return for this personal sacrifice, you may expect to get some satisfaction, productivity, or profitability out of these little gray boxes. And some folks actually do…the folks who sell them.

In the meantime, the rest of the world simply gets sucked

in to high-tech, and some folks get sucked in too deep. They spend way too much of their precious time at a keyboard, ignoring much more important life-events like mowing the lawn or giving the cat a bath. This can have a serious effect on a family, to the point that everyone feels neglected and depressed, except maybe the cat.

That's why you need to be aware of the tell-tale signs of computer obsession. Some people stop sleeping because of computers. Some people stop dating because of computers. Some people stop dating because they're dating computers.

Have you gone too far? Your best friends won't tell you. Your boss won't tell you. Your spouse won't tell you...she probably won't even talk to you unless it's through a lawyer. Get help before it gets this bad. Recognize the signs of computer addiction, before it's too late.

The Symptoms

Are you up all night talking on the Electronic Highway? Are your office, car, and bedroom filled with diskettes and manuals? You, or someone close to you, must be able to spot the symptoms of addiction. There are ten clear-cut warning signs. Memorize them...or better yet, see your doctor.

1. You spend half your time talking to your spouse about computers.

2. You spend half your time talking to your computer about your spouse.

3. No matter which hotline you call, they all recognize your voice.

4. You keep a laptop in the bathroom, instead of the Sunday paper.

5. You become an expert at PC Solitaire.

6. Your monthly phone bill is greater than your modem's baud rate.

7. You know your computer's birthday.

8. You make your family celebrate your computer's birthday.

9. You won't use another appliance in front of your computer.

10. You rust-proof your PC, or at least try to get it Scotchguarded.

☺

Getting Help

Once you realize you've got a problem, the first step is to get help. You don't have to go to therapy. Your computer doesn't have to go to therapy. You just need to take small, gradual steps, and there are lots of options.

1. CUA (Computer Users Anonymous). This is the organization for computer addicts on the brink. These folks nervously share stories of over-the-edge obsession and desktop-till-you-drop dependency.

And at the end of every gut-wrenching session, a CUA counselor passes around a laptop, encouraging each participant to touch it; even hug it if they must, and then pass it on. It sometimes gets a bit rough watching three or four reforming addicts trying to pry the device loose from the clutches of a tormented and wimpering sufferer...but curing computer addiction isn't pretty.

CUA meets once a week in a local church or civic center; check your phone book for a CUA near you.

2. High-tech Hypnosis. There is a new and growing opportunity for "Certified Hypnotists for Information Professionals," otherwise known as CHIPS. They offer videos, audio cassettes, and one-on-one sessions, constantly repeating and reinforcing subliminal messages like, "I will not touch a keyboard, I will not compile, I will not steal passwords from the Pentagon, etc."

High-tech hypnosis is an private, confidential, and effective way to start treatment for computer addiction. Of course, if you suddenly find yourself taking out the garbage, volunteering to do your spouse's laundry, or spending more time with your in-laws, you may want to check if someone close to you is messing with the messages on your tapes.

3. Professional Organizations. If you're still caught in the spiral of addiction, there are groups that actively recruit addicts. And while not attempting to cure them, they do try to put these folks to productive use while providing a supportive environment, a regular paycheck, and even a nice desk without any sharp objects.

If you are desperate and have no where else to turn, look these folks up in the Yellow Pages...under "Management Consultants."

Cutting Back

Rather than quitting all at once, you can also try to cut back on your computer usage. Maybe try to get down to a diskette a day, or just one or two spreadsheets between meals.

You can also try to substitute common household items for your computer. Slowly kick the habit by spending an hour a day using something else. Why not an electric typewriter, for example? Or pound on a piano for half an hour? Your fingers will keep busy, but you may chase away a few family members until you learn to play the thing.

If you miss your mouse, why not get the dust off your old Ouija Board? It moves around like a mouse, and a bunch of computer addicts can use it at once. Or you can try to find something else around the house that's shaped like a mouse, such as a horseshoe crab…there's usually one or two handy.

Finally, instead of sitting in front of a computer screen, try sitting in front of the TV. Millions of people spend an hour or eight a day watching TV with no unpleasant side-effects… except maybe an unusual affinity for salad spinners, ginsu knives, and 28-song record collections from those super 70s.

Cold Turkey

Maybe you've had enough. Maybe you're tired of being tired, having clothes smell like diskettes, and sitting in the computing section of restaurants.

So if you're brave, cut the cord. Just quit, cold turkey. Never touch a keyboard again. Hundreds have done it, and you can too. There are Computer-free Clinics, where your withdrawal is closely monitored by trained physicians. Or some doctors recommend the transdermal computer system, known as the Silicon Patch.

Whatever the case, total withdrawal is drastic. But those

who survive say it's worth it; it's worth living computer-free. Give up your gigabytes! Forsake your floppies! Leave your laptop, and use your lap for more important things.

TWELVE

A Final Warning

Psychologists have proven that humans are born with three natural fears:

1. the fear of falling,
2. the fear of loud noises, and
3. the fear of computers.

There has also been some debate about a fourth fear: the fear of anchovies. But not wanting to offend anyone in the fishing industry, let's just stick with the first three.

Due to this innate techno-fear, it is therefore counter-instinctive, if not downright impossible, to use a computer. I have tried my best, however, to offer you this step-by-step, chapter-by-chapter method, so that you may be free of your computer inhibitions.

But let me now warn you: I have a pretty bad track record when it comes to inhibitions. I suffer from dozens of them, especially the handful that are associated with using a restroom alongside ninety-five other people at half-time.

Even worse was the time I convinced my fiancée to take-up skydiving, a sport to which she had a rather sensible aversion. I will long remember the Saturday we rented both plane and pilot, planning to fling ourselves and our inhibitions out the door at several thousand feet.

Regrettably, at the appointed moment, I jumped...she didn't. I wound up with a rather bruised pelvis, she wound up with the pilot; they're now married and live in Tucson. And to make matters worse, the afternoon cost eighty bucks and she'd promised to pay me half.

But all that is in the past. You must now, without question, overcome your fear of computers. Your success in the world, both present and future, depends on your tolerance for all the accuracy and inadequacy high-tech has to offer. From finance to fast-food, everything you do from this day forward will require the components and consent of computer systems.

Is this scary? Yes. Is this dangerous? No. You've got to believe me, computers are really rather safe and trustworthy.

In fact, there is only one documented case of a computer catching fire and exploding, and that was in Minneapolis in the winter of 1986, when someone used one to try to jump start their pickup.

So it is now up to you. You can learn to live with computers, stay abreast with technology, and reap the benefits...or you can be left behind. The prospect of being left behind is very unappealing. Although I'm sure there was a time, long ago, when people really didn't use computers. I have a vague recollection of being alive back then, and all I remember is Junior High, girls and acne...mostly acne.

But if you do a little research, you may find someone old enough who lived through several of those technology-deprived decades. It's gruesome to imagine, but these folks were forced to co-exist with such torturous devices as rotary dial phones, ice cube trays, and TV's which made you get up to change the channel.

These people doubtlessly lived with hardship and misery. No fax machines. No car phones. No cable TV. But thanks to high-tech, we've got all this today, and more. We've spent mega-billions on computers. And now we have more hardware and software and networks and cables and consultants than you can shake a joystick at. It's scary how fast, smart, and powerful PC's are today. I have more on my desktop today than there was in the whole city just a few decades ago...maybe that's why I can't find anything.

But strangely enough, my life doesn't seem any easier. I'm always in the office till way past six. I'm still just a half-step ahead of my bills. I've got more than my share of high-tech gadgets, but traffic is still the pits, I'm losing my hair, and there's never enough hot water in the morning.

With all these computers, am I any better off? Old-timers insist that high-tech hasn't changed a thing. They'll tell you computers don't make people happy…cheeseburgers make people happy. Cheeseburgers, and M&M's, and weekends at the ball game.

These things were around before computers. Maybe they'll be around long after computers are gone. Personally, I haven't given the matter much thought. I've got no time for weekends at the ballgame. I've got a computer, and I spend most of my time figuring it out.

Here's hoping your system is up, your software is friendly, and your computer is kind. Good luck.

Glossary

alphanumeric   The numbers and letters you try to key into the system.

alphamoronic   The number and letters you actually key into the system.

binary   A string of 0's and 1's, which a computer interprets either as a software instruction, or a really embarrassing bowling score.

boot up   The term for what happens when you turn on a computer and it works like it's supposed to.

boot down   The term for what happens when you turn on a computer and it doesn't work like it's supposed to, so you kick it off the desk.

downsizing   Getting rid of your seven-foot-tall mainframe so your company can use powerful, less expensive computers.

downsqueezing   Getting rid of your seven-foot-tall mainframe through a 6' 8" computer room door.

E-mail   Electronic mail, which lets your computer act like a post office box...except you don't get letters from Publishers' Clearinghouse, or any carpet cleaning coupons.

IBM compatible   How a salesman describes your PC just before you buy it.

IBM combatible   How you'd describe your PC once you try to use it.

input   The stuff that goes into a computer, like time, sweat, money, a spilled thermos of hot chocolate, etc.

K	Means "one thousand." When you buy a PC, it comes with a certain number of K. If you pay a little more, I think you can get Special K.
LAN	When you spend enough money so that all your workstations can talk to each other, you have a Local Area Network. When you don't spend enough money, you have a Local Area Notwork.
logon	The first thing you do with a computer.
logoff	The next thing you do with a computer, if you've got any sense.
microchip	The expensive piece of technology that is the "brains" of the computer.
mochachip	The flavor-of-the-month that dripped down the back of the computer, probably on all your microchips.
monochrome	A one-color screen.
nonochrome	A broken one-color screen.
multi-task	Performing many tasks at one time, such as fixing a jam in the printer while reading instructions on fixing a jam in the printer

	while realizing your two-year-old is pouring jam in the printer.
printegration	This is when your instructions say your system can connect to other systems, but no one has a clue how to make it work.
response time	The time the system "waits" just after you press ENTER. Usually measured with a calendar.
spreadsheet	The complicated budget model you entered into the system, which is going to make you look really smart at the big meeting.
shredsheet	The budget report that finally comes out of the printer, five minutes before the big meeting.
stand alone	What a computer person does at a party.
taxes	What most people try to do with their computer.
taxes	What the IRS audits with their computer, and their computer is much bigger and smarter than your computer.
user-friendly	What you wanted.
user-fiendly	What you got.